Easy Pumpkin Carving

Spooktacular Patterns, Tips & Ideas

Colleen Dorsey

With carving patterns by Llara Pazdan

D1416485

FOX CHAPEL
PUBLISHING

Introduction

Welcome to a brave new world of pumpkin carving and embellishing. We've all carved pumpkins as a kid, or carved pumpkins with our own kids. So why this book?

First of all, in these pages you'll you find the tips and tricks you need to make pumpkin carving easier, faster, and more effective than the carving you might already know how to do. With tons of useful info about types of pumpkins, carving tools, pattern usage, and more, your next pumpkin will blow your old pumpkins out of the water!

Second of all, this book will teach you several techniques for carving and embellishing pumpkins that go beyond traditional carving. You can create luminary pumpkins and etched pumpkins, combine multiple pumpkins in creative ways, and embellish pumpkins without even touching a knife. It won't be until you see the ideas presented in this book that you'll realize just how cool (and easy) pumpkin carving can be!

So turn the page and get ready to have the best pumpkins on the block this autumn.

Contents

Types of Pumpkins

There are many kinds of pumpkins to choose from when it comes to carving and embellishing. What you choose will depend on what kind of project you want to make. Here are just some of the main options!

- **Standard pumpkins:** Your typical pumpkin is big, orange, and sturdy. This is a go-to pumpkin for any project! Common varieties include Cinderella and Jack O' Lantern (yes, that's a real type of pumpkin!).

- **Mini pumpkins:** Tiny pumpkins have variety names like Jack-be-littles, Munchkins, and Baby Boos, and they are just as cute as their names. These little pumpkins aren't as easy to carve, but they're perfect as fall foliage décor accents, and they can be painted or embellished with very little material or effort.

- **White and gray pumpkins:** Depending on what you do with a white pumpkin, it can be creepy—like a ghost!—or elegant. Whatever you choose to do with it, white pumpkins are definitely a welcome departure from the norm. The Lumina variety in particular is white on the outside and bright orange on the inside, giving a very cool effect when carved.

- **Other colored pumpkins:** Pumpkins come in many other colors and patterns, like blues, greens, stripes—you name it, it probably comes on a pumpkin! Each variety is slightly different, so do a little research before attempting to carve a pretty pumpkin you're not familiar with.

- **Gooseneck gourds:** We can't forget good old gourds! The unique shape of a gooseneck or swan gourd, with their long necks and stems, is a treat to work with for embellishing techniques.

- **Knobbly/warty pumpkins and gourds:** These are a challenge (or next to impossible) to carve, but the allover bumps are really eye-catching. Try incorporating them into your design!

Choosing High-Quality Pumpkins

Picking your particular pumpkin is important! Buy one with **smooth, unblemished skin**—no cuts or dents. If you want the carving process to be easier, pick a pumpkin with **one flat side** to carve on. A nice, **uniform color** means a pumpkin is ripe, and that's what you want. To test if a pumpkin is too old, press your thumb up on the bottom; if it's soft or pokes through, that's not a **fresh pumpkin**!

TIP: Don't be afraid to purchase a pumpkin with an irregular shape. Sometimes a weird shape can positively affect the personality of your pumpkin!

Traditional Carving Tools

Here are the main tools you'll need for carving a traditional pumpkin. As you dive deeper into this book, you'll encounter more specialty tools for specific techniques, but the ones listed here are commonly used for traditional and other types of carving.

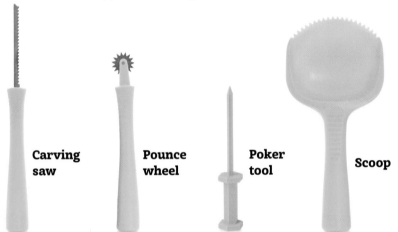

Carving saw **Pounce wheel** **Poker tool** **Scoop**

Carving saws or knives: Typical pumpkin carving kits come with a few serrated saws with teeth of varying sizes. Larger teeth are good for cutting the lids off of the pumpkins and for making big carving cuts. Smaller teeth are good for cutting fine details and doing precision work. If you don't have pumpkin carving tools like these from a kit, you can use serrated dining knives from your kitchen. Just be careful, as the grips on dining knives are not as secure as saws made for pumpkin carving, and some kitchen knives can be very sharp indeed.

Poker tool or pounce wheel: A poker is like a little skewer with a handle; you use it to poke pattern holes to follow while carving. A pounce wheel is like a mini pizza cutter; it will make lots of little shallow holes to follow while carving. Both will poke through paper patterns, so both tools will do the job of transferring a pattern to a pumpkin!

Scoop, ice cream scoop, or big spoon: Scoops made for pumpkin carving and ice cream serving are easiest to work with because their shape allows them to dig into the flesh of the pumpkin more effectively, making removing the pumpkin guts a quicker process. They also have more comfortable handles because they are made for the repeated scooping motion. But you can certainly use a normal big spoon from your kitchen if you don't have a scoop.

Other Helpful Materials

Work surface and accessories: In general when working with or carving pumpkins, you need a **sturdy piece of furniture** to work on, not a flimsy folding card table. You don't want the table to shake while you're sawing away at your pumpkin! You will also probably want some kind of **protective paper or plastic** to cover your surface and make cleanup easier. Just be sure to tape down anything that might shift on your work surface, especially if you are carving. You can also try cutting a piece **non-slip drawer liner** to create a non-slippery surface to work on. Just discard it when you're done! A pair of **rubber gloves** is also a useful accessory, whether you just use one glove to help keep your grip on the pumpkin while you carve, or whether you want to keep your hands and fingernails clean while you scoop out pumpkin guts.

    Candles and lighting tools: You can play with fire by using real candles, or play it safe with battery-powered ones. If you're using real candles, select a small, squat candle that won't easily be knocked over, and use a long lighter or slide a long match though the pumpkin's face instead of reaching all the way in through the top of a pumpkin with a lit match.

Using Patterns

Before applying a pattern to any pumpkin, you should prep the outside surface of the pumpkin (see step 1 on page 10). If you are planning to do a traditional carved pumpkin, be sure also to scoop out the pumpkin guts (see steps 2–3 on page 10) before using the pattern.

1. SIZE AND CUT THE PATTERN.

Use the pattern as is or photocopy the pattern to the size you need for your pumpkin. If your pattern is in two halves, use tape to assemble the halves into a complete pattern. Trim around the edges of the pattern with about ½" to 1" (1 to 2.5cm) of space around the edges.

2. ATTACH THE PATTERN.

Start taping the pattern to the pumpkin where desired. Use scissors to add little snips along the wrinkled edges to help get the pattern as flat as possible against the pumpkin's curved surface. If you're a beginner carver or it's an advanced pattern, you may want to attach the pattern to the flattest side of the pumpkin.

3. TRANSFER THE PATTERN FOR TRADITIONAL CARVING.

Once the pattern is attached, punch a series of holes into the pumpkin through the pattern paper, following along the lines of the pattern. If the design is very complicated, poke all the dots, remove the pattern, and go back and draw light pencil lines connecting the designs, using the pattern as a reference.

4. TRANSFER THE PATTERN FOR OTHER CARVING OR EMBELLISHMENT.

Alternatively, if you aren't cutting your pumpkin traditionally (all the way through or at all), there are other pattern transfer options. Try cutting out all the individual elements of the pattern, taping each one to the pumpkin, and tracing around them with pencil. You can also test out using an orange dry erase marker (or other washable marker), which should erase easily. You can also try to freehand the pattern directly on the pumpkin by looking at the existing pattern for reference; sometimes this is necessary anyway if the pumpkin has a peculiar shape that doesn't match the pattern you like!

Traditional Carving

Here they are, the very essentials of pumpkin carving! By following these steps that you probably had down pat when you were a kid, you can get carving with any traditional pumpkin carving pattern. You'll need a little elbow grease and a tolerance for mess to use this technique, but it's totally worth it.

Pre-Carving Pumpkin Prep

1. CLEAN THE PUMPKIN.
Prep the pumpkin first by rinsing it in cold water and using a scrub brush to remove dirt. If you want, you can spray the entire pumpkin with a mild bleach and water solution to kill mold and bacteria.

2. CUT OUT THE LID.
Use a sturdy knife to slowly and carefully carve out and remove the lid of the pumpkin, going in at an angle rather than straight down in. Alternatively, you can cut a hole in the bottom of the pumpkin, which will mean you can sit your pumpkin on top of a light rather than placing a light inside the pumpkin.

3. CLEAN OUT THE GUTS.
Use a scoop to completely empty the inside of the pumpkin of flesh and seeds. Keep scraping away at the inner walls of the pumpkin until you only have about a 1" (2.5cm) thick pumpkin wall that is nice and smooth.

4. ATTACH THE PATTERN.
Transfer the pattern using your desired method according to the instructions on page 8.

Carving Tips

Actually carving your pumpkin is simple enough. Here are some tips to make carving easy and effective:

- Saw steadily with a continuous up and down motion, and don't press too hard or try to go too fast.

- When you're finished cutting out a standalone piece (like an eye), pop it out of the pumpkin wall with your finger, not your carving tool.

- To cut clean, sharp corners, remove and reinsert the carving tool.

- Carve starting from the inside of the design and working your way outward.

- Resist the urge to put your free hand inside the pumpkin while carving. Only do so if you can clearly see where all of your hand is.

- If you accidentally break off a part of your carving as you work, such as a protruding tooth, stick it back on with a toothpick!

Preserve Your Pumpkin!

Keep your carved pumpkin cool and out of the direct sunlight (you can even put it in the fridge). You can also coat the interior and all cut edges with petroleum jelly to help lock in the pumpkin's natural moisture, or purchase special preservative sprays for pumpkins.

Don't be afraid to carve simple faces in little pumpkins! They can be super cute.

This amazing carving works with the pumpkin's skin for a creepy effect. Plus, it adds etched elements (see page 16 for more information about etching).

Try using oddly-shaped gourds and working with the shape of the gourd to make the faces.

Try using toothpicks as teeth.

A pumpkin's stem can easily be made into its nose, as shown here!

Making Luminaries

You've seen them before: luminaries are usually made of punched metal or paper bags and are lined up along sidewalks or driveways. But pumpkins make great luminaries, too! (Before beginning, follow the Pumpkin Prep steps on page 10.)

Special Tools

You'll need a power drill with either a spade bit (which are inexpensive) or a Forstner bit (which will make cleaner holes), or an inexpensive power rotary tool (see page 17 for more information).

1. SECURE THE PUMPKIN.

For this technique, since you are using a power tool, it's especially important that your pumpkin is solidly placed and won't move as you work on it, or slide out of your grasp. (See page 7 for tips on a secure work surface.)

2. BORE HOLES.

Following your pattern, drill holes along the pattern lines as needed. Most standard patterns will look best with evenly-spaced holes. However, some patterns, especially abstract ones, might look interesting with variable distances between the holes (imagine a swirling nebula with densely-placed holes near the center that are spaced farther apart near the edges).

3. CLEAN UP.

Go back to each hole and use a cotton swab or other handy tool to make sure you've knocked all of the excess pumpkin flesh out of each hole.

JENNA BUNNELL FROM VIDENDAE, WWW.VIDENDAE.COM

Use Different Bit Sizes

Experiment with using the same kind of bit but in different sizes to make variably-sized holes.

KATHY WOODARD AND STEVE BATES FROM THEGARDENGLOVE.COM.

Try Adding Lights!

If you're really feeling ambitious, cut a hole in the pumpkin's rear bottom and feed a string of LED lights inside the pumpkin. Then push a single bulb partly out through each bored hole from the inside. This will take your glow to the next level!

TECHNIQUE 3:

Etching

For a truly artful pumpkin, try etching. With this technique, you carve away most of the outer surface of the pumpkin, leaving a thin layer of pumpkin flesh intact. When you put a light inside the pumpkin, it makes the leftover thin layer of flesh glow! (Before beginning, follow the Pumpkin Prep steps on page 10.)

Special Tools

You'll need a small carving gouge or linoleum cutter. You can also use an inexpensive power rotary tool.

1. SECURE THE PUMPKIN.
For this technique, since you are moving your carving tool (or power tool) parallel to the pumpkin instead of into the pumpkin, make sure your pumpkin is solidly placed and that your hands and fingers gripping the pumpkin aren't in the danger zone too close to where you are etching. (See page 7 for tips on a secure work surface.)

2. MARK THE ETCHING AREAS.
Roughly color in each area that you want to etch out with a dry erase marker so you can see each shape. This is especially helpful if you have lots of little areas to etch out, because you might get mixed up and start etching an area that's meant to be left intact!

3. OUTLINE THE ETCHING AREAS.
Use your carving tool to scrap away the topmost layer of pumpkin skin along all of the edges of the spaces you want to etch, outlining each area clearly. Use light pressure and just worry about visually outlining the areas, not going deep.

4. ETCH THE AREAS.
After each etching area is complete outlined, start slowly removing the skin in each entire area. Remove a thin layer at first, then go back over the same area and remove more of the flesh. Work slowly and carefully—you don't want to accidentally push all the way through, and it's more secure to remove many thin layers than big, deep chunks all at once.

Using a Power Rotary Tool

Be safe! If you're unfamiliar with using a rotary tool, be sure to read all manufacturer's instructions and practice using it before attempting to carve a pumpkin. Also, be warned—it can be messy! Especially if you're using a more powerful tool instead of a battery-operated one, you're probably going to fling some pumpkin juice around, so make sure you've covered all nearby surfaces and are wearing safety goggles. As for what bits to use, we recommend a ball-shaped bit, a cone-shaped bit, and/or a cylinder-shaped bit.

TECHNIQUE 4:

Multi-Pumpkin Projects

It's time to really think outside the box! Use multiple pumpkins of different sizes to create cool vignettes or full porch decorations. Get creative and use your imagination! Here are some ideas.

Get ambitious by putting a skull in a pumpkin head! Find a white pumpkin that will just fit inside an orange pumpkin, then split the orange pumpkin in half and carve a basic face on it. Carve a skull face into the white pumpkin and nestle it inside the split-open orange pumpkin for a totally chilling effect.

Carve a small hole in the bottom of a pumpkin to sit it right on top of the stem of the pumpkin below it. See how high you can stack them!

This isn't technically using more than one pumpkin . . . but it's using more OF the pumpkin! Instead of throwing out the guts you scrape from your carved pumpkin, why not utilize them as a humorous accent as shown here? Just remember to toss the guts sooner rather than later—this technique is a one-night deal.

Try stacking and etching (see page 16).

You don't have to physically attach two pumpkins to make a statement. Try following a theme or just carving pumpkins that are "reacting" to one another.

Put a small pumpkin (or other appropriately-sized fruit) in the carved mouth of a big pumpkin. You can really make a funny scene by giving each pumpkin an expressive face!

Embellishing

There are a lot of crafters and colorists out there who haven't practiced much (or at all) with carving tools. While anyone can certainly learn to carve, and carve well, there's also something to be said for using the skills and materials you already have at your disposal to embellish a pumpkin without ever touching a knife. Sometimes it's easier, quicker, and less messy—and sometimes it's not! But if you want to break out of the mold, go for it. Here are some ideas how.

Puffy paint works great on a pumpkin. Use it to write out whatever simple message you want to share.

Take a collection of pumpkins and color them all in one color scheme, including a mix of patterns, designs, and letters to spell out a word.

Metallic and pumpkins totally mix! Cover a pumpkin in metallic paint or polka dots. White pumpkins make a great base for the metal to really shine.

Take a pair of fake plastic vampire fangs and add them to a mini pumpkin for a creepy effect!

Let your artistic side loose by hand-painting a design on a pumpkin of any shape.

Lace looks great contrasted against the vivid orange skin of a pumpkin. Add a simple bow, or wrap the entire pumpkin in lace.

By dribbling paint or melting crayons on top of a pumpkin, you can make a totally modern and stunning creation.

Pick a color scheme and attach scrapbooking elements and other decorations to a pumpkin, following the scheme.

Here's a cool seasonal idea! Use a hollowed-out pumpkin as a flowerpot for some fresh flowers.

Vampire

FUN FACT:
The modern, fancy-dressing vampire was invented at the same time and place as Frankenstein—during the rainy, boring summer of 1816 on Lake Geneva in Switzerland. To pass the time, four writers had a contest over who could write the best ghost story. Mary Shelley wrote *Frankenstein*, and John Polidori wrote *The Vampyre*—the forerunner to Bram Stoker's Dracula.

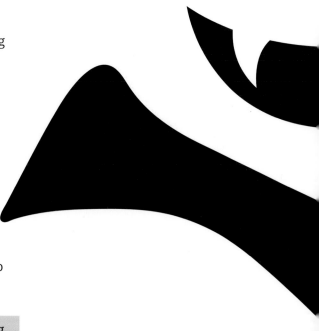

Best for **TALL** pumpkins!

Sugar Skull

FUN FACT:
While Día de
los Muertos and
Halloween come
at about the same
time of year, and both
make use of death
motifs, the two holidays
are very different! Tying
together Aztec rituals with
Catholic All-Saints Day, Día
de los Muertos has a lot of
meaning for Mexican people.
Colorful and fun, sugar skulls,
or *Calaveras de azúcar*, help
Mexicans remember their
departed loved ones with joy
rather than grief.

Best for **ROUND**
pumpkins!

Bat

FUN FACT:
Since ancient times, when caves were thought to be passages to the underworld, cave-dwelling bats have been associated with spirits of the dead. More recently, these nocturnal mammals have come to serve in the imagination as dark familiars: as cats are to witches, so are bats to vampires.

Best for **WIDE** pumpkins!

Creeper

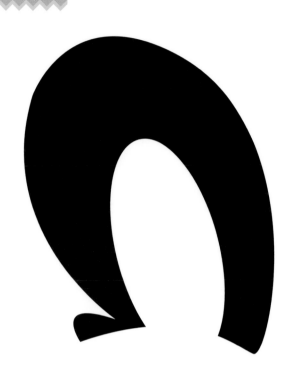

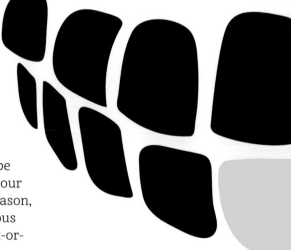

FUN FACT:
Halloween took on new meaning in the 1980s when slasher films, led by John Carpenter's famous *Halloween* (1978), dominated the landscape and left long-lasting marks on our imaginations. (For whatever reason, parents have been more cautious about letting their kids go trick-or-treating ever since.)

Best for **ROUND** pumpkins!

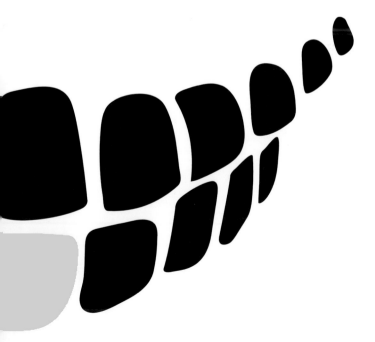

Black Cat

FUN FACT:
No witch is ever very far from her "familiar" black cat! In medieval times, when people were more superstitious, it was widely known that a black cat may very well be the devil in disguise!

Best for **ROUND**
pumpkins!

Witch on Broomstick

FUN FACT:
In the Middle Ages, witches—once thought to be helpful as well as harmful—got a bad rap. From the release of the witch-hunting manual *Malleus Maleficarum* in 1486 up to 1939's *Wizard of Oz*, witches (the bad ones at least!) were personas non grata in polite society. "Let the joyous news be spread: the wicked old witch at last is dead!"

Best for **ROUND**
pumpkins!

Owl on Branch

FUN FACT:
Though the owl is most often known as the "wise" animal, in other times the hooting of an owl at night was considered a bad omen. In fact, cultures as diverse as Shakespeare's England and Native American tribes share the latter belief. To the Apache, for instance, a dream featuring an owl was a sure sign that death was on its way.

Best for **ROUND** pumpkins!

Scary Greeting

FUN FACT:

Whether or not you believe in ghosts, human culture has been thinking of them for a very long time, from the Old Testament to *Hamlet* to *Ghost Hunters*. We can't get enough of them! In fact, the appeal of confirming the existence of ghosts is so strong that people have been holding séances and doing "ghost hunting" exercises for over a century.

Best for **WIDE** pumpkins!

Ghosts & Ghouls

FUN FACT:
Not a ghost, not a vampire, but similar to a zombie, the ghoul is a monster we don't hear too much about. The word "ghoul" comes from the Arabic *ghul*, a monster that hung around cemeteries and out-of-the-way places, waiting for unlucky wanderers to snack on.

Best for **ROUND** pumpkins!

Scarecrow

FUN FACT:
For young people, Halloween originally meant roving around with your buddies doing pranks. These shenanigans reached peak annoyingness during the Depression, at which point authorities attempted to settle young pranksters down with curfews and officially sanctioned Halloween parties. Eventually, all-American trick-or-treating replaced the pranking.

Best for **ROUND** pumpkins!

Falling Leaves

FUN FACT:
Halloween is not a traditional American holiday like Thanksgiving. Irish immigrants fleeing the Potato Famine in the middle of the 19th century brought Halloween with them, and for a long time, Halloween was viewed as just an Irish-American holiday. Not anymore—*everybody* loves it!

Best for **ROUND**
pumpkins!

Simple Faces

Best for **MINI** pumpkins!

Best for **MINI** pumpkins!

Easy Pumpkin Carving